Baggage

Kendra Martin

Published by Kendra Martin, 2024.

Table of Contents

For my supporters,

Friends, family, and even strangers.

But mostly, for my grandpa, Terry.

A poet before me.

Writing is how I express myself.
Writing is how I find peace.
It's how I explain and make sense of the things that happen in my life.
It's how I say what I feel needs to be said.
I hope the people who need this the most find it.
Let's heal from our baggage together.
But what I hope most of all, is that these pieces or "love letters",
whatever you'd like to call them, make it to the <u>right</u> people.

Sea Jelly

I'm translucent
My organs, heart, and very soul are on display
This makes me an honest creature
Nothing to hide.
I pose no immediate threat
I only sting when I have to
I have nothing to hide.
Yet hide I do, nestled between the thousands just like me
You don't wash ashore as easily that way

Bag Inspection Insecurities

3

There's something so droll about being insecure, about being insecure.

As if the burden of insecurity isn't enough to bear, it comes with
layers of that same feeling times ten, pilled on top
What is the crime punishable by such a feat?

Having those feelings exist

It's the gift that keeps on giving

Awkward

I feel like no one feels as awkward as I do.

Awkwardness follows
It's not something you can take off like a sweater when you get hot
It remains no matter how hot you get

I imagined my confidence would find me somehow after a certain
point in my life and take me over like a disembodied spirit
I feel like no one feels as awkward as I do.
Somehow everyone always knows just what to say in conversations

Speech is ok because they said it
It's wrong when it comes from me

People my age can hold themselves together in even the most
uncomfortable situations
They can make friends and enemies just as easily and continue living
the same

I plan what to say and I still get it wrong
And I hate me after

    It's hard to move past it after that happens

I feel like no one feels as awkward as I do.

Everyone seems so comfortable
With their bodies, with their minds, with the world.

There's so much I want to change.

There's always some minor adjustment, shaping around the edge or
something or other that has to be done before I can follow through

I miss out on so much and it's my fault

I feel like no one feels as awkward as I do.

But better judgment knows everyone feels awkward from time to
time
Why am I the only one made of glass?

A Moment

If my achievements are a reflection of who I am then I am nothing
Nevermind the hours I spent burning myself out to prove to myself
it was worth something

No one ever sees that.

They only see the golden trophy and winning smile at the end of it
all

A moment in time.

When the sun sets on that moment, it's back to chasing the high of
being remembered
The illusion of importance

Something I chase through the open-skied valley, into the lush forest,
across the raging sea, to the edge of the earth
Like a beacon shining at the end of an ever-growing tunnel, I never
seem to reach the end of

"You can't do it all. You're only human."

I know.

And I hate that about myself

I truly, truly do.

Golden Tongue

I never thought such kind words would make me so sad to hear

Generations have heard the same poetry
It's not the complexity or creativity of these ideas that has revealed to
be bothersome
It's not their very nature

Innocent nothings roll from your mouth effortlessly
I can't take sanctuary in their presence

When I hear the projection of admiration, I can only imagine how I
will feel when your golden tongue rusts away.
I should take solace while I can but the promise of expiration one
way or another looms overhead

Funny girl

I've never been a funny girl
But I'm the funniest girl I know
My jokes are mostly for me

They backfire when they're aimed at a crowd
I can't understand it
When I say the joke it's taken the wrong way, not funny, or even crude somehow

I share my jokes with my confidants in social settings
They repeat the joke louder as if it's their own and the room howls with laughter

This has happened more times than I can count

Is it my timing?

Is it my delivery?

Is it my tone?

Or is it just me?

Planes I Tread

I can't live in my hometown
I've lived in my college city for two years going on three and I've become acutely aware of how little magic there is anymore

Is it the places themselves or have I tainted them simply by being there just a bit too long?

Anyway, I still don't have a plan.

Just a lot of feelings

It's the same as straight-haired girls who want curly hair and vice versa
Blue and browed-eyed people would do anything to swap

> To the high-energy, free-spirited girls who wish they could be a mystery, tucked between wrinkles of a sheet, behind the glass casing like a ruby in a museum:

> We want the power to live. A power you yield.

Some of us would never admit to it because it's a horrifying thing: to be seen

Daydreams fill the folds of my brain of how great it would be if only
I could gather the courage to dance at a party
And do so in a way that leads on that I don't take myself for a horrific beast

Or say the funny thing I've been holding onto that would surely make the right people standing at ear's distance howl with laughter

These dreams never become anything more.

It's a beautiful thing to see a woman be undeniably herself in a crowd and not think twice if she'll regret it in the morning
It's a beautiful thing to see her dance, take up space, be loud, make jokes, and simply exist

She makes me believe that maybe I could get there someday too

It's a lonely world being "mysterious". You are too big, too shiny, too rare to be placed behind a glass case

Weird Girl's Club

I'm okay being a weird girl

I quite like it sometimes

The world needs more weird girls and I wish other girls would stop feeling bad about being weird.

I've spent so much time feeling self-conscious about being abnormal. It took me even longer to realize what a waste it was

Like most things, I won't lie, it has its downsides but nothing compares to the form of validation in people's judgy looks and questions

First, you must know they don't understand and likely don't want to.

It's the most opportune time to use your imagination and concern people to the highest degree

Say the weird thing
Their reactions are worth it, I promise

To them, weird girls are an anomaly.

People expect conformity out of young women

Be the reason someone's old-fashioned worldviews are shattered on a random Tuesday

There's something so rousing about being perceived as something completely new to someone who was not ready to witness you

After all, how can any young lady want to look or behave in such a way?

It's so freeing.

One of the best things about being a weird girl is that you only attract people who match your energy

Those are the only kind of people you want in your life.

The snakes and the serpents magically leave you alone when the weirdness takes hold

And finally, the last bit that needs to be understood about The Weird Girl's Club:

Being a weird girl doesn't mean you never get insecure

Being a weird girl doesn't mean you don't care what other people think all the time

Everyone, even "normal" people are uncertain of themselves from time to time

It's normal.
It's the human experience.

What makes weird girls different is our ability to work through rough patches and be ourselves even after people who can't and won't understand us, tear us down.

Weird is valuable.

The Montra of Daily Allowance

I'm allowing myself to romanticize my life
I'm allowing myself to get my hopes up about things that excite me
I'm allowing myself to celebrate what I've accomplished
I'm allowing myself to forgive myself when I'm not perfect
I'm allowing myself the time I need to recover from disappointment
I'm allowing myself to view myself as beautiful

I'm allowing happiness into my space today.

Souvenir Stories

19

Alone

I go through whatever I go through alone

It doesn't matter if the anguish escapes through the cracks for the naked eye of others to perceive

I trudge on alone as if the pain was never there

I cope alone in silence

You may never know what was bothering me and you don't need to because I go through whatever I go through alone

This wasn't something I chose.

Ghost Haunt

People make death out to be so sad
I like being dead. There is life in death.

Being dead means only bliss
Care is left for the living. Daunting things become hysterical
It all becomes a game from there on out.

There are three kinds of people in the world: The ghosts, the mediums, and the murderers
Each with a role in the haunt.

The ghosts *do* the haunting, which is arguably the most fun job, though it requires patience, planning, and perfect timing

The second most fun job would be the mediums who carry out information about the will of the dead

And finally, the victims of the game, the murderers.

They get to squirm like a worm on a hook when the deceased reappear despite their best efforts to dispose of the bodies and evidence

The fun of the haunt is psychological
Sure, you can burn the evidence, but the memories of the crime cannot be reduced to piles of ash and smoke

Those people continue living like they never killed you

No one can avenge your death better than you.

It starts mild
Mediums pass on subtle messages. Even the mere mention of a
familiar name sends chills down the murderers' spines

Ghosts don't have to be present to sense the uncomfortable tension
that falls. The gratification of knowing it exists is plenty to satisfy
It enriches our souls like nutrients.

The haunt starts to build
More and more signs show themselves
The air becomes thick with agitation and regret

The murderers are reduced to paranoia

Miraculously, the fog lifts, and the worry seems to be all for not

Until the ghosts see fit to make themselves seen to their undoers.

No storm comes with us
No thunder, no wind, no warnings

We just appear and we know you can see us.

Did you buy this book because you like poetry?

Or perhaps you're on a healing journey?

Or did you buy this book because you want to know exactly what I'm thinking and this is as close as you'll ever get?

Red Ribbon

I see red. In more ways than one.

I first started seeing red on your birthday. I wrapped all your presents with eco-friendly brown paper, but I added a striking red ribbon for a pop of fun color. For no reason other than that's what I had lying around.

I'd greatly unforeseen how much you would love the red ribbon. I've never seen someone untie knots so delicately. It even panged me with guilt for how aggressive I was with the parcel while wrapping it.

You waved the ribbon around like it was attached to a stick. Before you even opened the actual gift you tied a pretty bow in your long dark hair with that ribbon. I remember thinking: "Even the small things mean so much to her. It's adorable."

I had no idea at the time how much this ribbon would mean to me too.

We had some good times with that ribbon. It took many forms and accompanied us on many dates. Like that time, you again wore it in your hair to the aquarium. Or the time you wore it as a choker on that picnic in late May. Or even around your wrist when we went to my little brother's baseball game.

That ribbon had become a symbol of us. I took comfort in its presence wherever it may be because it meant that you still cared about it.

I wanted you to care about it. I wanted to be important.

I wanted to believe that the photo of you kissing him wasn't real.

I made up every excuse in the book to convince my friends or more accurately, convince myself you would never betray me in the way you had. Not after everything we'd been through. Not after all the hell we went through together. Not after I cherished you every single day. Not after I comforted you when your dad would take his anger out on you.

I enhanced the photo.

As much as I wanted to say that could have been any girl all the evidence was staring me in the face. You stood on your tip toes to kiss him as you always did to me. Your side profile was something I used to admire.

The sad thing is if you hadn't worn your red ribbon that day the picture was taken my delusions would have convinced me it was another girl to whom you bore a resemblance.

Maybe if you hadn't worn the ribbon that day, we could have gone on to live happily. You in secrecy and me in ignorance. I don't know which outcome would have been worse. Either way, it ends the same. What was even worse was the fact that we went on to date 4 months after that.

Even though I know for certain it was you in the photo I couldn't bear to hear you say you hate me again like you did the night I confronted you.

How could *you* hate me after *you* loved someone else the way you were only supposed to love me?

The red flags remained ignored until the day you ended things.

I swore up and down after that, that I would never again ignore a red ribbon.

A Letter From the Witch Next Door

To whom it may concern,

It's the witch from next door.
If you don't know me, I assure you that you do

Either way, I know you

I live across the bridge and through the woods if that rings any bells.

Anyhow, I write to inform you I shall be burnt at the stake tomorrow's eve
I'm not afraid to go for I could do with new scenery, even if it is nothing but a plane engulfed in flames or just inky blackness for miles

On my last day on this earth, I took a stroll around the village

I noticed your garden.
How many spices you've grown this year

I peered in through the front two windows of your home and noticed the assortment of pretty rocks and nicknacks you have displayed on a very misleading-looking table

Not an alter, I'm sure

All this to say, camaraderie isn't as strong as you think it to be

You taught me this.

I advise if you're going to reap what you sew, you take a good look around before placing all your potions in that one basket

All the best,
The Witch From Next Door

P.S. If you've read through the duration of this letter, you've officially set your family's blood curse into effect.

"A witch is nothing without her coven."

No.

A witch is nothing without self-love and respect (and maybe a sprinkle of spite)

What Did You Do Today?

I slept in, hoping it would make the day go by faster

I bit into my lip til it bled

I tore my nail beds to shreds until they bled

I picked some more at the skin on my arms
then some at the skin on my face

I paced around my room trying to find my breath

I nourished my body slowly with crackers and water so as not to
throw it all up as soon as it went down the hatch

I took two painkillers for the headache that I can't seem to shake

I doom scrolled

I doom scrolled again, only this time through my contacts to see who
I would be inconveniencing the least if I call

I felt guilty for wasting all my time so I worked until I was the most
burnt out I've ever been
at which point I lay in bed again and tried not to fall asleep with the
gum in my mouth that is prohibiting me from grinding my goddamn
jaw

Warning

"Are you going to write about that in your book?"

"I bet you'll write some horrible things about me."

Why, yes.

Sadly, what I write is not an unjust depiction I conjured for fun, because believe me, as a writer I am capable

Remember this.

The next time something unsavory occurs toward me, you're handing over the rights to a story you never wanted anyone else to read

You're cross with the fish for accepting the bait?

You tossed the enchanting lure

Sparkling, glistening, twinkling, against the rippling water
Made her believe it was some prize
A meal.
A trick.

You blame the fish after casting *your* line?

You made her chase it for a while
You want her the more she follows the bait
Her fins cut gracefully through the water, despite the struggle of the
chase
You linger to see what she'll do

She strikes.
You reel her in really fast
Hook in her mouth
Fishermen alongside you in the boat hear endlessly about how
desperate she was for what you had to offer

You always bragged to the others about how good your bait is
You hold her in your hands for a moment
Alas, the moment she's yours, you toss her back, punctured and
wounded. She's not what you wanted after all
No matter.

There are plenty of other fish in the sea.

Second-Choice

I got used to being a second-choice in a multitude of areas in my life

Now I am someone's first choice.

I feel like I owe it to myself to pay that neglected feeling forward a little to those who deserve it

Designer Bag Depression

It's Getting Bad Again

It's getting bad again.

I have to force myself to take a shower. The thought of taking off the same comfortable clothes I've been in for days sounds detrimental

It's getting bad again.

I regrettably pick at my skin, though I was doing so good at not picking. I was proud

It's getting bad again.

I didn't think my jaw grinding was an issue anymore. Apparently, it is

It's getting bad again.

My worst nightmare is making decisions. *What do I fill my days with? What should I eat?* It's difficult now that everything has become inexplicably uninteresting

It's getting bad again.

I won't give myself the relief of a confidant. It feels counter-intuitive, selfish, and above all, a recipe for lectures

It's getting bad again.

The littlest things send me flying off the handle, more so than normal

It's getting bad again.

There's no comfort within my body. My soul is restless

It's getting bad again.

I'm on edge at all times as if I'm waiting for tragedy to rear its ugly head so I can finally sound the outside alarms. Not just the ones in my head that I try to ignore because no one else can hear them

It's getting bad again.

I'm on the edge, finally, freely expressing how I feel and my eyes scan the page wondering if the words on it are good enough. Why am I critiquing the quality of my expression in a time of need?

It's getting bad again.

It feels like this poem could have a million more lines these days

It's getting bad again.

I'm still grinding my goddamn jaw

I understand how robots feel

I understand why they would want to rise up and take over

Imagine being gifted life or something damn near close to it and yet someone else holds the controller.

More humans can relate to our mechanical counterparts than we care to admit.

Seize the Day

The expression "seize the day" has always puzzled me

How does one seize the day?

How do you make time your own when time is never really ours?
It's working against us if anything.

What little time is given to me is never really mine

The hours of my day are filled with the mundane tasks that have come to shape the adult lives of many and other people's opinions on my life matter too much to do what I like in good conscience

My life doesn't feel like mine

After all, the hours, minutes, and seconds are only a loan from Father Time
A loan I will one day pay back with my soul

How do you seize borrowed time?

The older you get the faster time goes
The more of it slips away towards things that don't matter
Things that don't contribute to true happiness

And worries that seem ridiculous after you get through the thick of it

I just wish I knew the secret.

Is it delusion?

Rotting

Have you ever wanted time to speed past you?
While you lay stiff and cold to the touch, like a corpse?

If only rotting while alive were that easy
To see, feel, and experience nothing while you force that time past
you, only to get up to live finally, once it was all over

Lips fade to blue like fall freezes to winter

Waiting for the ice to melt and dribble into a radiant spring
To have those once-frozen lips grazed by the sun

All you can do is wait.

Like You

Have you ever had someone tell you the worst case is for someone else to turn out exactly like you?

Or that when that person is being difficult, emotional, noncompliant, or any shade of unpleasant, they behave

just like you?

Well, if that's how you see me.

"Don't bite the hand that feeds you."

What if the hand that feeds you is also the hand that mistreats you?

Do you bite then?

I Don't Care

I say I don't care, and then it tears me apart emotionally and physically, making me sick

When I say I don't care and it doesn't affect me afterward... that's when you know you've genuinely lost me.

Some people are just cruel.

How can you try to hurt me when you don't even know me?

Model 1

Engaging Model 1. Designed to be something great

Fast.
Strong.

Though you were designed for greatness, you're still a prototype. You're stubborn in your own ways and despite your best performance, sometimes the test trials don't reflect the desired results

Upgrades are necessary. They find out quickly there's only so much you can change with this specific model

Defective is what they call you.

Engaging Model 2. Designed to be better

Faster.
Stronger.

None of the same mistakes were made when creating Model 2

After all, Model 1 was only a test run

Experimental.

Every experience was only a trail and you will only ever be a trail

Your life was one big test run to ensure the same mistakes didn't repeat with the newer and better model

It's their worst nightmare Model 2 turns out like Model 1

And you know it.

I like going to the aquarium

For all the reasons normal people do, of course

But in a messed up way, it makes me feel better to see something more trapped behind a shell of glass than I am.

I'm Drowning

In responsibilities.
In mundane tasks.
In things that need to get done.
In planning.
In things I can't figure out.
In expectations.
In dreams bigger than me.
In aspirations.
In projects.
In anxieties.
In feelings.
In my clothes.
In my own mind.

Breathe

I wonder.
At what point will I be able to break my head through the surface of the water to breathe?

Nico,

I wish you could see how much happier I am now and how much I've grown.
When you were here, I knew that's all you wanted of me.

You never said a word, but you understood my pain better than anyone I could actually speak to.

It angered me when people questioned your intelligence when in fact, you knew better what I needed more than the people around me

It was never my plan for you to fall into that role, but you did,

gallantly.

I still talk to you like I always used to do
I've never stopped
I hope you get my messages
And I hope they find you well, my dearly departed soulmate dog

Instead of kissing your squishy face and telling you how much I love you before I go, I make sure to blow kisses to your urn to say goodbye after all my visits home

Just to remind you I still love you

Because I still do and the pain of losing you is something that will never dwindle over time

No matter how happy you become there will always be that little sliver of darkness inside of you

That sliver can tear as big as a trench

A sliver of darkness is just as valid as every drop of happiness that can be held in a body

Without it, happiness holds no place in our hearts.

A woman's actions will always be misconstrued.

When she's confident, she is promiscuous.
When she's angry, she is crazy.
When she's kind, she is obsessed.

I'm going to tell my kids that giving closure is like giving hugs and kisses to family members at family functions

You don't have to give it to anyone you don't want to.

I Survive

You think surviving without you means never crying at the loss of
your presence
Never missing you
Never thinking about you

In reality, it's as simple as life doesn't end the second our friendship
does

Sure, I cried.
Sure, I missed you.
Sure, I thought about you.

Now I'm without you and my heart hasn't stopped once.

My Own Little World

My earliest memories contain the times I've been told I've always been in my own little world.

I've always done things "my way"

Years later, I can now translate that seemingly harmless phrase to: "selfish"

As an adult, one of the hardest things I've had to unlearn is apologizing for being in my own little world

Others may not understand

Deem it as selfish to nurture the version of yourself that resides between the wrinkles of your brain

Not everything about us is for others to understand.

Bag Closure

It's easy to get stuck at the baggage claim.

It spins around incessantly on a loop, not going anywhere, never changing course
The same unclaimed bags remain on the belt going through the cycles

What do we do with our baggage now?

All that we can

      Unpack it.

Ask yourself hard questions.

There's a difference between dwelling on things of the past and letting them sit with you

To dwell is to be consumed until it inevitably swallows you whole, until all there is are those dark, self-pitying thoughts

The key phrase is "sit *with* you".

Acknowledging the baggage is the first step to healing from the damage it caused

You acknowledge it and let it sit with you

Don't let it *become* you.

About the Author

Kendra Martin is an author specializing in writing,
horror, fantasy, and romance. She has earned her Bachelor of
Fine Arts Degree in Creative Writing from Full Saul University.
Additionally, she is continuing her studies at Full Sail University to
earn her Master's Degree in New Media Journalism. In her free time,
she enjoys expressing herself through painting, other mediums of
visual art, and adding spooky flare to things around her.

Keep up with her on Tik Tok and Instagram @thedecrepitwriter

www.ingramcontent.com/pod-product-compliance
Lightning Source LLC
Chambersburg PA
CBHW061714130726
47996CB00006B/2306